An Autism and BPD Story

Asten Clarke

Dedicated to every single person
who is autistic and/or has BPD.

Introduction

I have decided to re write my life story. Not that there was anything wrong with the first edition, I just felt there could have been so much more detail in it.

Why did I decide to write my life story at such a young age? The truth is, while I'm only twenty-eight, I have been through more than the average twenty-eight year old. Because I am autistic, and I have Borderline Personality Disorder (BPD).

I also wanted to write my life story because I am a writer. I've wanted to be many things in my life, but being a writer seems to suit me because I can do it on my own terms.

It's been difficult writing down my life, and I've had my work cut out trying to remember everything, but if it helps just one person, it will have been worth it.

I hope you enjoy reading my story.

Asten x x x

Chapter One

Childhood

I was born on Thursday September 3rd 1992 at Ipswich Hospital. I had some health complications at birth. I'm not sure exactly what happened, but I know I was very ill. They put me in an incubator that was way too small. The lack of space caused trauma with my brain.

I came out of hospital at two weeks and went to live with my mum and biological dad. I can't remember much about this particular time. My mum and dad split when I was two and my mum married my step dad when I was three. I was their flower girl. I don't remember much about the wedding, other than that my mum had to cancel the balloons she'd ordered as decorations because I was scared of them (more on that later.)

I got diagnosed with mild cerebral palsy (CP) as a baby and, after a lot of hurdles, as autistic at the age of four. I was a complex case because I mostly presented as someone who was 'high functioning' (even though I now know that functioning labels are pretty useless), but also had some symptoms common with 'low functioning' kids such as spinning.

I had a happy childhood. Given the chance I would definitely go back. As a kid one of my biggest passions was music. I always wanted to be a singer as a kid and even wrote one or two of my own songs, which are pretty embarrassing looking back. My love of music goes back to before I can even remember, when I used to sing along to my mum's tapes in the car. Then when I was about four or five I started to develop my own taste in music. My fave band was the Spice Girls. I had loads of

Spice merchandise including CDs, videos, dolls and even a toy mobile phone (I don't know why this sticks out among everything else). I even went to see them live when I was about five or six, but like a lot of things around that time, I can't remember much about it. I do remember going to playgroup one day and singing loads of Spice Girls songs in the talent show when all the other kids sang nursery rhymes. This again is a little embarrassing looking back.

Another thing I loved as a kid was Barbie dolls. I had two or three boxes full (not including accessories!) and I played with them almost daily. It was fun creating stories for my dolls to take part in, although I did get a little pissed off when I lost one of their tiny shoes, which was often!

I had some weird phobias as a kid. One was, as mentioned before, balloons. I don't know why i was afraid of balloons, but I suspect it had something to do with the loud noise they made when they popped. Another phobia I had was The Muppets, and again, I've no idea where this came from. In the 90s there was a batch of Disney VHS tapes with a random Muppet short at the end, and I seemed to have all of them! It really freaked me out. I remember begging my mum to turn the tape off before the short came on. It's bizarre.

Another fear I had, one that affected me quite a bit, was saying people"s names, including my own. I also couldn't say the word 'balloon' for obvious reasons. I've no idea where this fear came from. It wasn't until I was about fifteen that I was able to overcome this fear. And much like the fear itself, I have no idea how I was able to overcome it.

I found out I was autistic at the age of nine. Apparently I took it really well. I've always thought of my autism as a good thing, well, apart from when I have meltdowns.

Speaking of meltdowns, they happened pretty often during my childhood. They could be triggered by anything from a playdate with one of my cousins ending to not being able to come up with an idea in English class (again, more on that later.) These meltdowns are not something I'm proud of, and although they still happen now, they are much less frequent.

When I was ten I was invited to a group for 'high functioning' autistic kids at a local special school. While I was there I struck up a friendship with the only other girl in the group, and it was then that I realised that autistic people really are all different. We were like chalk and cheese. I was into pop music and stuff; she'd never heard of any of the bands I'd listened to. But the biggest difference was that she could write stories and at the time I couldn't. I don't know why this was, but I suspect it was because I didn't have the confidence to write.

Through this friend I met another best friend called Katie, who became one of my bestest friends ever. She had Ehlers

Danlos Syndrome and her joints would regularly snap out of place. I remember she stayed over at my house once and I think she dislocated her shoulder or something. Nevertheless she got on with it and after it snapped back into place she was her happy bubbly self.

My passion for music continued into my tween years. I got really into S Club 7. I used to watch their TV show and I had all their CDs, I even got to see them in concert a couple of times.

I had other special interests during this time. I used to love

Cartoon Network, particularly The Powerpuff Girls. Again I had lots of merchandise and I even dressed up as one of them once.

But my biggest special interest during this time was a show on the CBBC channel. It was called The Basil Brush Show. I watched it one day on a whim and totally fell in love with the main character. Quite literally. I told my parents I had my first crush. Needless to say they weren't exactly pleased and tried to blame my then best friend for 'putting silly ideas in my head'. But the truth is, this obsession has never gone away, in fact it's only gotten stronger. More on this later on. (I'm gonna be saying that a lot, I can tell).

I found school really tough, like a lot of autistic kids. It wasn't so much the subjects (well, apart from English), but the other kids. I tried to make friends with a group of girls in my class, and when we were moving up to high school we actually requested to all be put in the same form group, which we were. But cracks started to show when one of the girls started saying her mum knew Lee Ryan from the boyband Blue. To this day I'm not sure if she was telling the truth or not, but one of the other girls seemed pretty convinced, and this drove a wedge between them and the other girls in the group. Another thing that happened was... well, boys. It seemed the boys in our class hated me, and were forever tormenting me in ways such as kicking my backpack on my back, etc. My 'friends' seemed to want to impress these boys so they stopped hanging out with me. One day it all got too much, and I had a massive meltdown. But guess what happened? *I* got kicked out of school, *not* my bullies. Typical.

With nowhere else to go, I ended up back at the special

school full time. I really didn't enjoy my time there; I was the only girl in the group and I felt really out of place there.

Chapter Two

Teenage Years

As I went into Year Nine I started going to a Pupil Referral Unit (PRU) three days a week. The PRU only held about thirty students and was for troubled teens who had dealt with issues such as bullying etc. I noticed some of the other kids were a bit more rebellious than I'd been used to. They smoked, they drank (although not on school premises), and seemed to be quite troubled.

But I really enjoyed my time there, felt like I fitted in and couldn't wait to start full time in Year Ten.

In Year Nine we did a limited schedule of activities. We did English, maths and science. We also did a session called Jigsaw. It was called Jigsaw because there were four parts to it - singing, dancing, guitar and drumming - and in the end we would all join together for a performance. You could choose which group you wanted to be in and I chose singing. For the first couple of weeks we just did karaoke, and then we started working towards our first performance, which was the Christmas Bazaar. The Bazaar would be held at the school in the evening and there would be stalls selling things there. (I remember I also designed some Christmas cards to be sold there). And then at the end of the night we were going to do a performance of *Winter Wonderland.* In the March the following year came our first major performance, the Celebration of School's Music at a venue called Snape Maltings. As the name suggests we weren't the only school to take part. We took the whole thing very seriously and started rehearsing as soon as we got back after Christmas. The first time we did it we did sort of a 'music through the ages' sort of thing, starting with an ancient African chant and ending with a rap. We had a lot of fun, and when we did the show we even had a dressing room! I remember thinking that was really cool.

Speaking of music, during this time something unbelievably exciting was happening within my family. My cousin Scott is a singer, and he got put into a boyband called Avenue. The band auditioned for the X Factor and got through to the finals, but unfortunately they got disqualified for already having a manager.

They ended up releasing a single, Last Goodbye, and I can't remember where it got to in the charts but I know it got to Number One in Scotland. My mum and I had fun following them around as they did their promotional tour. We even got to go to their launch party! It was an amazing experience.

I never told anyone at school about my cousin. I don't know why; I guess I didn't like the attention.

In Year Ten I started full time at the PRU, and there were some new students joining us. One girl who particularly stood out to me was called Laura. She was, and I realise I'm about to quote Mean Girls here, 'like the Barbie doll I never had.' Except I had a lot of Barbie dolls. I thought Laura was the definition of cool. She seemed so much more grown-up than me, even though she was actually two months younger. She was also really pretty, and even did some modelling once. I wanted to be just like her. This is probably where my BPD symptoms start showing up because, and I'm ashamed to say it, I got a bit obsessed with Laura.

In December we did another Christmas Bazaar, and that meant

another performance. This time we sang All I Want For Xmas Is You by Mariah Carey, and this time we performed to the karaoke backing track. I don't know why we did that, but I suspect it was because it would be a hard song to learn on drums/guitar.

In January the weirdest thing happened. There was a new student, called Callum. At first he was just one of the other kids, but then I got chatting to him. And I started to fall for him. Hard. I told him how I felt after a while and he said he had kind of guessed (was I really that obvious?). He also said he wasn't interested in any kind of relationship. Not just with me, but with anyone. Like me he was autistic, but unlike me he didn't like to be touched.

We did Snape again in the spring. This time round we wrote a couple of our own songs, which was fun. Afterwards we had an award ceremony at school. I can't remember what award I won, but I think it was for effort. I won the chance to make my own CD. I sang 'Everytime' by Britney Spears. That was a great experience.

The final year at school was pretty eventful. In the December I was thrilled to be invited to

Laura's 16th birthday. I was actually invited to her birthday and her party. On her actual birthday we went to her house and sang karaoke. And then the following Saturday she had rented a pink limo and we all got driven around town in it before going back to her house for drinks. I didn't drink alcohol back then and felt a little out of place because Laura and all her friends did. It wasn't that I wasn't allowed, I was just scared. Of what I do not know. But I don't think Laura minded.

Towards the end of the school year I had a bit of a disagreement with Laura. I had sent a message to her boyfriend on Bebo (these were the days pre-Facebook). I didn't see anything wrong with it because I'd met him and spoken to him at the party. But Laura didn't see it that way. She and her mates launched a campaign of abuse towards me. It was all online over MSN and Bebo, but I was still a bit scared to go to school.

I did still go to school obviously. I was taking my GCSEs at the time and really wanted to get good grades. I was so relieved on the last day. We didn't have a prom because it was such a small school, but we did have a party to celebrate us leaving, complete with an awards ceremony. All the awards were personalised for each student. I won the award for 'Pop Star of the Year' because of my love of singing. I hadn't spoken to Laura since the argument over the internet. So I was really surprised when she came up to me during the party in an effort to make up with me. I hate any kind of confrontation so I accepted. I still talk to her on Facebook sometimes.

Chapter Three

College

I passed my GCSEs, not with flying colours so to speak, but I got three C's and two D's, and that was enough to get me into college. I chose to study Art and Design. I'd always enjoyed being creative so taking an Art course seemed like a good idea. I had dabbled with the idea of Music and even Childcare, but I figured I'd enjoy Art the most.

I did a wide variety of projects in my first year, from painting and textiles to animation. But my favourite subject area was Graphic Design. For my final project in the first year I designed a magazine for autistic students. The people at the college liked it so much that they asked me to produce it for real. So I got a team of my fellow students together and we got started on the first issue.

But while I was at college, I was dealing with a personal issue at home. After being afraid of them for so long, balloons had become a special interest for me. I remember thinking I was weird, that I shouldn't have this fascination for them, at least, not at my age. Another thing I always seemed to have a fascination for was sex. And one day I found myself on a sex education site for teens. There was an article on there about fetishes, and it briefly mentioned balloons. I figured that was what I must have; a balloon fetish.

I didn't think much more about it until I found myself on YouTube one day, and found videos of women - fully clothed - blowing up balloons. I put two and two together and realised I'd stumbled upon my first fetish videos.

Then at the age of fifteen I read an article in my mum's magazine about 'looners'. This was the first time I'd come across the word and it definitely would not be the last. The article featured various women talking about how they liked to play with balloons sexually. They explained that, within the fetish, there were 'poppers' and 'non-poppers'. Pretty self explanatory, I think. I identified myself as a non popper.

At the age of sixteen my parents bought me my own laptop which I was at first allowed to use in my bedroom. And since I was alone for the first time, I decided to Google 'balloon fetish'. To say I found a lot of stuff is an understatement. Among all the porn sites (which freaked me out a bit, if I'm honest), I found a forum called UK Looners, which I instantly signed up to. Even though I was only sixteen and not even allowed. But I was young and naive; I didn't realise.

On the forum there would be discussions about balloons and the latest balloon videos. These would be, as mentioned before, videos of women blowing up balloons. Well, naturally I wanted a piece of the action so to speak, so I posted a few clips of myself onto Youtube. I managed to get some balloons that were kept in with the rest of the party supplies. I turned on my webcam, blew them up and posted the video to Youtube. The comments came in thick and fast. Looking back I think it's all a bit creepy and sick, given the fact I was only sixteen, but back then the attention felt so good.

Then I got a message on Youtube from a guy called Craig. He said he was a 'fan' of mine and asked if we could talk on MSN Messenger. I accepted, and he asked if he could send me some balloons. Now, I'd done the Internet safety lessons at school and knew the dangers of giving out my personal info online.

But on the other hand, I was running out of balloons. So I gave him my address.

Some time later the balloons arrived. My parents found the package and demanded to know what was inside. They already knew I liked balloons but didn't know quite how much. So I said, 'just open it'. I don't know if they were shocked or what but they demanded to know who it was from. There was a note inside the package, of course, and it read something along the lines of, 'I hope you enjoy these balloons as much as I will enjoy watching you with them'. God, why couldn't the ground just swallow me up right there and then?

After they discovered the package my parents insisted that I use the computer in a communal area. So I could hardly do stuff in plain view of them.

The balloon stuff went on for about a year first time round, and during this time I also had my first boyfriend. Actually, scratch that. I did 'go out' for a bit with a guy online from Birmingham but it didn't work out. But this was my first real boyfriend. It was a blind date set up by my mum and her friend. After our date (I can't remember what we did), we decided to start going out. It was cool because he could drive and that's something that hasn't happened since that relationship.

But unfortunately it didn't work out. He dumped me by text! Said he wanted to spend more time with his friends. Later he admitted that he had been making passes at me but I hadn't noticed. More on that later (again.)

I don't know what made me stop doing the balloon fetish stuff the first time round, but to say that time was eventful is a vast understatement. I was a member of a social group called Out & About, which was a charity for disabled teens. One of the cooler things we did was a project with ITV Fixers, which gives young people the chance to speak out about issues that they feel passionate about. Our project was called 'We Can Do It' and it was all about disabled teens doing the same things able bodied/neurotypical teens can do. We had a film crew come in a film us doing activities like bowling and shopping. And then we had a disabled actor from EastEnders come in and talk to us about... well, being a disabled actor. That was all filmed as well. Part of the mini documentary was shown on the local news, and I got all my friends and family to watch.

That summer my friends Sadie (who's unfortunately no longer with us) and Becca were going to Movie Camp. I wasn't going but of course I wanted to be with my friends. So they managed to get me in on a day pass kind of thing. It was at this camp where I would meet the love of my life, Myron. He asked me out on the first day and I was a little apprehensive at first, but there was something about him that I really liked. We spent the rest of camp getting to know each other, and by the end of camp I had invited him to my eighteenth birthday party. On the night of my party, we started going out for the first time.

Then in November the scariest night of my life. I was due to go to a fireworks display with Myron and before I was due to go my family were having a Chinese takeaway. Up until this point, I hadn't ventured far past chips, but tonight my mum suggested I try a chicken ball. So I did. Big mistake.

My throat started to close up. I thought I was choking at first. My parents only live down the road from the hospital so we got straight in the car and drove there. The doctors rushed me into a room and started giving me water etc and when the swelling didn't go down they asked me if I was allergic to anything. My mum said I was allergic to peanuts. So they gave me an adrenaline injection and the swelling went down immediately. I'm usually scared of needles but the allergic reaction was a million times more scary than any injection! I thought I was going to die. I went to college the following Monday because I was adamant I didn't want to miss it, but I ended up having a massive panic attack and had to go home. Since then I've had countless panic attacks, feeling like my throat is closing up again.

The following year I had my first smartphone and I decided to join the balloon forum again. I thought that now that I was eighteen I could handle it. How wrong I was.

This time I was more vocal about my interests and posted a Basil Brush fanfic I had written on the forum. I got a message from a guy who called himself Stealth Dragon, and I don't know how it happened but we started role playing together. Stealth Dragon was American and so didn't know about Basil Brush but I educated him about him.

There were some other new names on the forum. One couple who particularly stood out to me were known as Loon Master and Red Fairy. Loon Master was the one with the fetish and his wife Red would play along. Red also had some videos on Youtube of herself playing with balloons. I don't know why I got obsessed with Loon Master and Red, but I suspect it was because I wanted to be an independent adult like they were, and I wanted a relationship like theirs.

Chapter Four

Sectioned

I never intended to leave home when I did. I thought I would be there for at least a couple more years, but when I left the house that day, I never returned home permanently.

My memories of that day are a little blurry. I remember sitting at home with my support worker, and I was desperate to get on the balloon forum. I managed to get on there, but something on there triggered me. I don't know what it was, but I think it had something to do with a magazine article Red had recently done about the balloon fetish, and i'd left a comment, and someone must have replied to it.

I can't remember what I did, but it must have been pretty bad because when my parents came back they managed to get some respite for me for a few days. This of course meant no internet for a few days. Not something I was happy about.

Anyway, the first night in the respite house went ok. I had a decent bedroom and there was a

TV downstairs. But the second day - 11th June 2011 - I was just desperate to get onto the balloon forum. Again this is very blurry. I remember completely trashing the whole house. The police were called, and I was arrested. I'd never been arrested in my life and I was so scared. The handcuffs were really tight and hurt my hands when I moved them. I was taken to the police station and placed in a cell, where I spent the majority of the day. I was scared, upset, bored.... And I just wanted my mum. Being questioned by police was pretty scary too.

Eventually I was released, but I didn't go home. I was sectioned under the Mental Health Act and placed in a psychiatric unit.

Looking back, I'm not sure this was the best thing for me. At the time I just accepted it, but looking back I'm not sure it was something I needed.

The unit was full of colourful characters. Some of them really freaked me out. I'd love to paint mental health units in a positive light, but the truth is I did not enjoy my time there.

Some people were nice though. I made a few friends, but

never kept in touch with any of them.

Red's article came out a few days into my hospital stay. My mum was reluctant to buy the magazine for me, but she did anyway. I don't know why she did, but I ended up reading the article over and over, memorising the words and poring over the pictures. She looked so glamorous and I was very jealous.

I had lots of visitors when I was on the unit, including Myron. We'd just got engaged and were planning to have a party to celebrate. I was worried I would have to stay in the hospital and we wouldn't be able to have the party. Myron has learning difficulties and so it was difficult for him to understand what was happening to me. I felt bad for him, like it was somehow my fault. I still feel like that about that time to an extent.

I had art therapy and counselling while I was on the unit, but didn't really feel like they were helping very much. They said there wasn't much they could do for me because I was autistic, which is pretty ridiculous really. If only I'd known about BPD then, things might have been so different.

About halfway through my stay at the hospital, we were going to be moving to a new, more modern building on the main hospital site. Surprisingly this move went really well and didn't disrupt me too much.

One of my college tutors came to visit me on the unit. She had been helping me run the magazine. But she came with bad news. I wasn't allowed to come back to college, and since I wouldn't be at college, the magazine would be changing hands to other students. I was devastated.

I was allowed some home leave now and again and on one occasion I stayed with my grandparents. We talked about how the unit wasn't really helping me in terms of my mental health, and was literally just somewhere for me to live because I couldn't go back to living with my parents. So I had an idea. I asked if I could stay with them while I was being found a suitable place to live. Luckily they agreed, and the hospital said they were happy to discharge me if I had somewhere to go.

I was discharged on 22nd August. I know this because it was

my brother's birthday. We celebrated by taking the dog for a walk by the seaside. It was lovely to spend time with my family again.

I lived with my grandparents for about two and a half months. Quite a few things happened during that time. I didn't have Internet access at home so I was making daily commutes to the local library (and needless to say they got to know me there!). I had a free bus pass so it didn't cost me anything. What did cost me was having to pay a pound for every hour I wanted to use the computer after the first two, and I could be on there all day sometimes, because I was still addicted to the balloon forum at that point.

Then one day on the forum (which for some reason wasn't blocked at the library), Loon Master made an announcement that he and Red Fairy were going to hold a balloon fetish party, the first of its kind in the UK. Of course I wanted to attend, but the party was hundreds of miles away in Birmingham. Plus with the comments made about the magazine article a few months before, Loon Master and Red didn't really like me that much. OK, that's an understatement.

They hated me. So I had no chance of going to the party.

But then, I don't know how it happened, but I was given an advocate. His name was Jonathan, and he was an older man. He was involved in the kink scene and was a member of the social networking site Fetlife which Loon Master and Red were also members of. He said that he would talk to them for me. Unfortunately he had no luck, as Loon Master wanted nothing to do with me. But then he said that he would accompany me to a local 'munch', a gathering of people interested in kink. I said that would interest me very much, but I think the only reason why I was interested was because Loon Master and Red were into BDSM, and at the time I was trying to be like them, which is a borderline symptom known as 'mirroring'. Anyway, it never happened. My mum made a complaint about an advocate taking a vulnerable young person to a 'sex club', and Jonathan was removed as my advocate.

Chapter Five

Moving to St Neots

It took social services a good couple of months to find me a suitable place to live. After all, I couldn't stay with my grandparents forever. The first place they found me was a place in Norfolk. It was kind of a hospital, but I instantly got bad vibes from the place and refused to live there. Back to the drawing board.

The next place they found was a care home in St Neots, Cambridgeshire. When we went to have a look around I instantly felt at home. It was very homely and the staff and residents seemed nice. They'd even put a spread out for lunch especially for me! Even though it was about sixty to seventy miles away from home, I agreed to move there.

I moved in on 15th November 2011. My parents helped me move in, which was a good thing, because I would have a three week induction period where I couldn't talk to them. I met my key worker, Ashley, who I instantly liked. She was only a few years older than me and we shared some similar interests.

The house was part of a care company, and there was another house next door that was part of the same company. The house I lived in held about seven residents in all. I was one of only two females in the house. I didn't get on amazingly well with the other girl; it wasn't that I didn't like her, we were just very different.

I was happy to have my own bedroom and en suite bathroom, especially because I would be sharing with so many males.

During the first week I went for a walk with Ashley into the town centre, to get acquainted with the place. It was quite a bit smaller than Ipswich, with only one high street and not too many shops. The shops it did have were mostly charity shops and coffee shops. On that day I signed up to the local library, because I still didn't have a computer at that point. Soon I was walking in and out of town every day just to use the library, and needless to say I lost quite a bit of weight. At one point I was down to a size six. (Oh. to be a size six again!)

I did many different activities when I lived in St Neots. Some with other residents and some on my own. One time we did a group outing to Alton Towers, and another time we went to a safari park. Solo activities included singing lessons, where I gained a Grade 3 in singing. One of the more exciting things I did was go on holiday to Disneyland Paris with Ashley.

I was still with Myron when I moved to St Neots, but the long distance thing put a strain on our relationship, so we decided to break up. I was gutted.

I had weekly sessions with a psychologist. The first lady I had was an Australian woman, but I didn;t really get on well with her.

Then I had a much younger lady who was much better for me, however I didn't think the psychology sessions were helping me that much. This is probably because I hadn't been diagnosed with BPD then.

Speaking of BPD, I was still trying to copy other people, particularly the balloon people. I saw them having what seemed like success and I wanted a taste. I set up my own balloon fetish clip store (I don't know how I got away with that), and I attempted to run a looner party. I failed spectacularly of course, and was shunned by the whole community.

I attempted college a few times while I lived in St Neots. The first time I went to Bedford College to do Graphic Design. I can't remember what happened but I quit before Christmas. The second time I wanted to do something different, so I went to Huntingdon College to do Childcare. This time the girls on my course (and it was all girls) were not very mature at all and they could sense I was different. Their bullying ultimately led to me withdrawing from the course.

During this time I had some extremely sad news. I'd just come back from being my cousin

Shelley's bridesmaid at her wedding, which I really enjoyed. I was getting ready to go to college the following Monday when my mum called me, telling me that my friend Katie had passed away. I was in shock. I didn't cry till that evening. It was the first time I'd lost someone close to me, but it would not be the last, as you'll see in later chapters.

Life goes on. This was shortly after Myron broke up with me so I was feeling kind of lonely. So I decided to try online dating. I met this guy called Mikhail. He was a few years older than me and lived in the neighbouring town of

Sandy. After talking for a few months we arranged to meet at Costa Coffee. I told him I needed to have a support worker with me but he seemed to be ok with this. We got on really well and found that we had a lot in common. We liked the same dance music and Disney movies, and decided to get together.

Around this time is when I decided I wanted to be a writer. I'd tried so many things (including trying to set up my own balloon decorating business while I was living in the care home!) but writing seemed to work for me because I could do it on my own terms. I knew online of a few people who had self published their own books. I decided this was the route I wanted to go down. They say 'write what you know' and that's exactly what I did for my first book, Rainbow Balloons. It follows eighteen year old Anna Jones, who is autistic, who unknowingly goes to work for a balloon fetish site. I was really proud of the work I did on that book. I don't know how many copies I was expecting to sell, but I know a few people read it.

As my relationship with Mikhail progressed he started coming to my house to spend time with me. At first the staff didn't let us go into my room, which is understandable, but once they got to know and trust him we were allowed to go upstairs. We never did anything though, and there is a reason for that. I identify as asexual. That means I don't feel sexual attraction to any gender. And yes, if you're wondering, I'm still a virgin.

On my 22nd birthday Mikhail met my parents for the first time. They all came to the house to celebrate my birthday. My mum had got Minion and Minnie Mouse cupcakes made for me, and my dad did a little photo shoot of me and Mikhail in the garden. We got chatting as you do and conversation turned to the magazine I'd produced with college. My dad suggested I produce an autism magazine of my own. I took his advice and attempted to create 'Aspies and Auties' magazine. But unfortunately I didn't know what I was doing without the college's help. It didn't follow through in the end.

That month I attempted to go to college for the fourth and final time. This time I was studying Animation, which I thoroughly enjoyed. But the college was a long way from the house. I had to walk to the bus stop, get on a bus and then walk from Bedford bus station to the college, and even though I was relatively fit back then, it killed me with my CP. So unfortunately, after two weeks I had to quit again.

Then in November something awesome happened. I'd been following Basil Brush on Twitter for about a year, and he announced he was doing a tour. Of course I quickly bought tickets for me and Mikhail (and I'd asked him beforehand and he said he'd be happy to go with me.) I Tweeted that I had bought my tickets and then Basil direct messaged me inviting me to meet him! Of course I said yes. I'd only been waiting half my life for this moment.

The day of the show arrived in February the following year. Mikhail came to the house in the morning to pick me up and we got the train from St Neots to Peterborough. When we got to the theatre we just hung around for a bit until this guy came up to me and said, 'Are you Asten?' I just nodded. He then gestured for me to follow him onto the stage. It was amazing seeing it all empty. It turned out that the guy was actually Basil's puppeteer (sorry to ruin the magic guys!) When I met Basil I was totally starstruck and speechless. It was a great day, the show was brilliant and I had a fantastic time.

But sadly my relationship with Mikhail did not last. He knew about all the balloon fetish stuff and hated it. He tried to convince me that they were all paedophiles, and for a while I believed him. So much so that I wrote a whole blog post about it. This and many other things have driven a wedge between me and the community.

Anyway, Mikhail left me, but I guess it was a good thing because

now I'm back with the love of my
life!

Chapter Six

Back to Ipswich

I decided I wanted to return home after quite an emotional home leave at my grandparents. I just wanted to be with my family. The whole thing worked surprisingly quickly. A social worker from Ipswich came to see me in St Neots to tell me they had found someone to share a house with. I was used to sharing with lots of people so sharing with one person didn't seem too bad.

I met my potential future housemate, Kirsty, for the first time in November 2014. We went for a drink at Costa Coffee in Ipswich. We seemed to get on really well. We shared some similar interests so we had some common ground. I also met one of the support workers who would be working with me, because the care company was already taking care of Kirsty.

In the New Year we went to see the house we would be sharing. It was lovely. It was a decent size - not too big or too small, and it had a garden which was good because Kirsty kept rabbits. A lot of rabbits. At first I was unsure about sharing my home with so many animals, but I was sure I would get used to it.

Before I left St Neots in April 2015, the staff there organised a leaving party for me, which was really touching. I can't remember much about what happened at the party, but it was really emotional. It was especially hard to say goodbye to my best friend in the house, Matt. We'd got on really well and always had a laugh. We promised to keep in touch after I'd left.

On 7th April 2015 my mum, dad and grandpa came to pick me up from St Neots. It felt weird leaving the house for the very last time, knowing I wasn't coming back. But it was also very exciting. I was about to start a whole new chapter in my life.

Moving in took a long time. Kirsty moved in first, because she had to get her rabbit sheds built in the garden. Her boyfriend helped her move in. I got help from my parents (of course). I got a new double bed and I had a Frozen canvas to put up in my room.

Most of the furniture in the living room was Kirsty's, which was a good thing because I didn't have any of my own furniture. Also in the living room we had Kirsty's pet chinchilla Millie (RIP), who was the only animal in the house mostly. So living with the rabbits wasn't so bad and I even adopted one. I named her Elsa after the character in Frozen. Then I suggested to Kirsty that we name all the rabbits after Disney characters! She thought this was a great idea.

We did a few activities together. Kirsty was really interested in animals so we went to a lot of zoos and safari parks. Animals aren't really my thing but I still enjoyed myself.

At home we did a lot of arts and crafts. We made Christmas cards to sell at a local church fair. We also made cupcakes whenever we had an excuse to make them.

During the summer of 2015 I was having problems with my friend Sadie on Facebook. I can't remember what the argument was about; probably something silly. I think she didn't like the fact I was still doing the balloon videos. We said some really horrible things to each other, and I felt terrible afterwards. But when I went into town one day shortly afterwards, I saw her on the bus and she smiled at me.

Then one morning I logged on to Facebook, and I couldn't believe what I was reading. History had repeated itself. Sadie had passed away. I'd lost another best friend. Again I think I was in shock because I didn't cry for a while afterwards. And I felt even worse about the things I'd said to her. I hope she knew I loved her.

I'd always had problems being addicted to the internet, ever since I first discovered the balloon fetish sites, and this is where it all went wrong with Kirsty. I can't remember the details, but I remember smashing her TV. It wasn't my intention and I regretted it instantly afterwards. Needless to say she wasn't very happy. Kirsty has a history of being violent as well. I was hiding in my room after the incident, and she came up and put a pillow over my face. I was really scared, but more than that I was upset that I had upset her. Luckily the staff broke us up. I went to my grandparents' house for a couple of days, and during that time I took my first overdose. I took all the medication that had been sent with me in my overnight bag. I got rushed to the hospital where I stayed overnight.

Chapter Seven

A Place Of My Own

While I was in hospital I got a call saying I couldn't live with Kirsty any more, and that I'd been found my own flat in the centre of town. Originally they wanted to move me to Southend but my dad wasn't very happy about that, and then they managed to get a place in Ipswich for me. This move happened very quickly; I came out of hospital on December 1st and moved in on December 9th.

Even with everything that had happened with Kirsty, the day I moved out was extremely emotional. We promised we would remain friends. In fact our friendship is now stronger than ever.

The flat was really nice and modern. It had two bedrooms; one for me and one for my staff. When I moved in I had to sort out my own internet and phone. I felt really grown up doing that!

It was nice because the flat was right on the Waterfront. But the bad thing (or good, depending on how you look at it), was that there were so many fast food joints just around the corner, plus a Tesco. So much for size six. I must have put on about six stone. I've struggled to keep the weight off since.

In April 2016 I took another overdose, and the scary thing is I don't know why I did it. I now realise that sudden mood swings are a borderline symptom.

On that day I went to Bingo with my grandma as I had done every Saturday, and suddenly a massive wave of depression came over me. I just suddenly got up and walked out, went to Boots to buy two packs of paracetamol, and then to Superdrug to buy two more as you can't buy more than two at a time. I assume this is so people don't do what I was about to do. I sat in an alleyway and took nearly all the pills with a bottle of Orange Fanta. To this day the smell of Orange Fanta makes me feel sick. Anyway, I walked home, and on the way I tripped up, probably because I was really high. This really nice couple helped me up, but I reckon they must have known I was on something. I wasn't right. When I got home my support worker knew instantly that something wasn't right, and she phoned for an ambulance. I'm so grateful she was there or God knows what might have happened to me.

I got taken to hospital in the ambulance and we met my parents there. After I was assessed and everything, which took a good few hours, I was taken to a ward. I had to have four drips of antidote. I was in hospital for nearly three days. When I finally got discharged my dad told me he thought I was going to die.

Around this time I was told I was going to have to leave my flat. This was because of the damage

I'd done to the walls when I'd been frustrated. I didn't want to leave; I loved my flat. That night I self harmed because I was upset that I had to leave the flat. But luckily I was OK and didn't do any damage to myself.

Chapter Eight

The New House

It took the care company over six months to find me a new house, the house where I live at the moment. It's a lot bigger than the flat. My parents were initially worried because the stairs are very thin and steep and the bathroom's downstairs. I reasoned with them that I would be OK and careful with the stairs.

When I moved in I had to sort out my internet and phone again. This time I decided to go with Sky because I liked the variety of programmes available on Sky TV.

In the November, Loon Master sent me a message, accusing me of harassing him as one of my alters. Alters are alternate personalities, and they are common in BPD. These alters mainly show up when I go online, and when I'm on one of my alter profiles I literally feel like I'm this other person. Anyway, I tried to explain to him that I hadn't been on my alter profile in months, and he seemed to believe me. We got chatting and ended up striking up kind of a friendship. I was thrilled, not only because I hate any kind of confrontation but also because I was still a bit obsessed with him and Red.

In the January I started going to my grandparents' every other weekend. I loved going to my grandparents' because it gave me a chance to get away from my support workers. I would stay from Saturday until Tuesday. On Monday we would go shopping and I would buy crisps, which they would then reluctantly let me eat in my room. I'm a little ashamed of this now.

In March something happened that changed my

perspective on life. Loon Master hadn't been online in weeks, and when I asked him why, he told me that Red had taken her own life. I was stunned. I thought she had everything. Loon Master explained the reason why, and I won't go into it because it's not my story to tell, but it just goes to show that you really don't know what goes on behind closed doors.

The previous August I logged onto Facebook to some news. One of the looners I'd been obsessed with, Chris, had died. You might be thinking I was upset. Oh, no. Even though I was obsessed with Chris, I hated him. He had a lot of media attention because of his fetish and let the fame go to his head. I can't stand people like that. And of course, being borderline I took things completely the wrong way, sending malicious messages to Chris' friends and family. I'm quite ashamed of what I did now, but back then I thought he deserved it. As you can probably guess I got a whole load of abuse from people I didn't know. They told me to kill myself, and at that moment I felt like it.

The first anniversary of Chris' passing was coming up, and again, I messed up big time. I posted messages to a Facebook page he used to moderate. I got confronted by a girl called Carrie. Again she sent me lots of insults and I retaliated. She tried to reason with me, and again, hating confrontation I co-operated. I told her I was sorry and she said she believed me. I added her as a friend and she accepted. It turned out that Carrie was autistic too, and it was cool having a friend in America. Carrie quickly became my 'favourite person', a term used in the BPD community for when you obsess over someone. Which made what happened later a whole lot more difficult.

Christmas came around, and I was expecting to get some kind of gig tickets like I usually do. So imagine my disappointment when it came to dinner time, and still no tickets. That was until my mum handed me a small gift bag. In it were two tickets and a flyer for the pantomime Sleeping Beauty in Windsor. What was so special about a panto in Windsor, you ask? Yep. You guessed it. Basil Brush. I was so excited I cried. I also cried because I was ashamed. Ashamed that I, a twenty-five year old woman, was excited about seeing a kids' puppet in panto.

The show was in just over a week's time. My mum came round a couple of days later and suggested that I message Basil on Twitter to ask if I could meet him again. He replied pretty much straight away, saying he'd love to meet me again. Once again, I was really excited.

The day of the show came around and my poor dad was feeling ill. Nevertheless he still drove us for about two hours to Windsor. I'll always be grateful to him for that. The show was awesome, but it was nothing compared to what came afterwards. Me and my mum went round to the stage door, rang the buzzer and were let inside. Soon after Basil and his 'handler' Mike came down the stairs to greet us. I was so happy I cried. Mum cried too, because she knew how much it meant to me. Basil gave me loads of free stuff and I had a selfie with him. When we left I couldn't stop smiling. It might seem silly, but it was one of the best days of my life.

I went from being on top of the world to depressed in less than a month. It happened when I went to stay with my grandparents for the weekend. I would go round there and use their computer and for the most part I was OK. But on this particular night, I dissociated as one of my alters while talking to Carrie. My alter said some pretty horrible stuff to her. Obviously I couldn't convince her that it was my alter that said those things, so she said she didn't want anything to do with me.

I spent the next couple of months obsessing over Carrie, and I'm ashamed to admit that I kind of stalked her. I didn't mean anything by it; I just missed her friendship. But unfortunately she didn't want to know me, and felt threatened by me.

Chapter Nine

Borderline Crazy

I'd been single for almost two years by now and I wasn't interested in being with anyone. Well, there was one person I wanted to be with. Myron. I'd been in love with him since we broke up nearly five years ago. One day, he added me on Facebook, and we got talking. He told me he was doing a DJ set at a club night. So me and my ex-housemate Kirsty (who's still a good friend) went along. We had a really great time and the day after Myron sent me a message saying 'thanks for coming last night'. We got chatting again and he asked me if I wanted to go out. I was thrilled. He then said, 'should we change our relationship status?' I was even more thrilled at that! We started going out and have been together since.

I hadn't written anything for a while and was beginning to look everywhere and anywhere for inspiration. Then it hit me. I would do a spin off from my first book, Rainbow Balloons. The Popper is the same story but from Anna's balloon fetishist husband Mark's point of view. I published The Popper in October 2018 after roughly three months of hard work. Then I had an idea for another novel. The Fan follows sixteen year old Amber Williams as she travels halfway round the world to find her idol, Jonas James. This book was inspired by me being a fan of Basil Brush. It sounds silly, but hear me out. Jonas isn't very popular in England, where he's from, and I wanted to convey what it was like to be so into something people don't take seriously. I ended up writing four parts to the story and compiling them all into one novel.

On 5th September 2018, two days after my twenty sixth

birthday, my life was changed for the better when I was diagnosed with Borderline Personality Disorder (BPD). It started when I had an appointment with the psychiatrist. The appointment was about changing my medication, but within minutes of talking to me and reading my file, the doctor knew I had BPD. It was such a relief to know what was wrong with me, and it answered a lot of questions. My mum and I had always said there was something other than autism, and now we had some answers.

I'd been a huge fan of JLS since I saw them on the X Factor.

Well, actually, it was since they released their single, Beat Again. Anyway, when they broke up I was devastated, But then in 2018 it was announced that Aston (my namesake!) would be doing a tour called Rip It Up, which was focused on dancing after he appeared on Strictly. Harry from McFly and Louis Smith were also involved. I asked my mum to get tickets, and on my 26th birthday, she surprised me with VIP tickets, which meant I was going to be meeting all three boys! I was most excited about meeting Aston though.

The day of the show came around and I was soooo excited. We got to the theatre early as we were told to, and then we were let into the actual auditorium. Then when I saw Aston I was so excited I cried, haha. It was a great experience, I got a photo with him and I will always treasure the time I met him.

After the first time, we made it a tradition to go and see Basil Brush at Windsor every year. Well, that's not quite the way to put it; I insisted that we go every year! But my parents didn't mind. The second time around I also met Anne Hegerty from The Chase, who is also autistic. Again I cried, haha.

2018 was a great year. Lots of good things happened that year. But unfortunately, 2019 wasn't so great. I'd been going to bingo with my grandma for a few years now, and one night she rang me to say she wasn't feeling very well, and she wouldn't be going the next day.

Little did I know this would be the last time I spoke to my grandma.

I should have known something wasn't right. It's not like my grandma to not want to go to bingo. Anyway, the next day (or maybe it was two days later, I can't remember; this particular time is a blur), she got rushed to hospital and was on the critical care unit. She had diabetes and she hadn't been looking after it very well. On the Saturday I went out with Myron, but my thoughts were understandably elsewhere.

On the Sunday my mum came round to deliver the sad news. My grandma had passed away. I went up to the hospital to be with her after her machines were turned off. But as before with Katie and Sadie, I didn't cry till much later. My mum was in floods of tears and

I felt like an emotionless robot next to her. I felt so guilty.

I was due to go and see Basil Brush in Easter panto two days later, and I was wondering if I should still go. My mum said yes I should still go, as grandma would have wanted me to go and have fun. But I felt guilty all the time I was there.

Luckily Myron was there for me throughout this sad time, and I don't know what I would have done without him. He even came to the funeral with me, for emotional support.

Life goes on, I guess. But I was extremely close to my grandma and her passing was a huge shock to us all. I think about her every day, and quite often see her in my dreams. I guess that's my way of coping with things. My mum says I've done amazingly well. I don't know if I agree with that or not; I've just tried to get by during this sad time.

Chapter Ten

Who Am I?

Well we're coming to the end of my story. For now, anyway. I'm only twenty-eight after all.

As you can see, I've been through quite a lot. But it's made me a stronger person and it's made me who I am today.

I guess all that's left to do now is look forward to the future.

Thanks for reading my story. I hope you enjoyed it.

Asten x x x

Contact Info

Facebook page:
https://www.facebook.com/astenc
larke

Twitter:
@AutisticAsten and
@AstenWriter

Instagram:
@missastenkathleen and
@astenclarkewriter

Website:
https://www.astenclarke.com

Printed in Great Britain
by Amazon

37050401R00067